ASTBACK

22

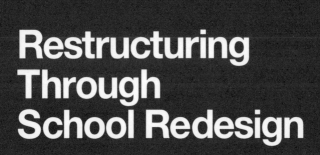

Restructuring Through School Redesign

Jerry Villars

PHI DELTA KAPPA
EDUCATIONAL FOUNDATION

JERRY VILLARS

Jerry Villars is currently a private consultant in schooling redesign, working primarily with school districts on implementing strategic planning components at the local school level.

For 19 years Villars served as a senior consultant with the Colorado Department of Education, where his responsibilities included coordinating the state's gifted child program and conducting school improvement workshops involving teachers, administrators, and the community. A former high school history and humanities teacher, he also has served as adjunct faculty at the University of Colorado.

Villars has designed curriculum materials for the 3-M Company and recently developed materials on schooling redesign for the Mid-Continent Regional Educational Laboratory. His publications include numerous articles on gifted child education, assessment of educational quality, and schooling redesign.

Villars received a B.A. in history and economics from Macalester College and an M.A. in history and Ph.D. in education from the University of Colorado. Additionally, he was selected to be a John Hay Fellow at Yale University and Education Policy Fellow at Georgetown University.

Series Editor, Derek L. Burleson

Restructuring Through School Redesign

by
Jerry Villars

Library of Congress Catalog Card Number 91-62116
ISBN 0-87367-322-0
Copyright © 1991 by the Phi Delta Kappa Educational Foundation
Bloomington, Indiana

This fastback is sponsored by the Suffolk County (New York) Chapter of Phi Delta Kappa, which made a generous contribution toward publication costs.

The chapter sponsors this fastback to celebrate the 25th Anniversary of the Phi Delta Kappa Educational Foundation and to honor its members' dedication to high educational goals and their service to the community.

Table of Contents

Introduction

It was Wendell Johnson (1956), the noted semanticist, who commented that giving something a new name might make it a new and different thing. He went on to remark, "A rose with onion for its name would never, never smell the same . . . and canny is the nose that knows . . . an onion that is called a rose." And so it is with "restructuring," a relatively new term in the education literature these past seven or eight years — a term that defies precise definition yet serves as an interesting example of the "rose/onion" conundrum.

For many, the term "restructuring" is merely another fad, a buzzword, a means of packaging and marketing school improvement in upscale language. Its most familiar referents include site-based management, collaborative decision making, school choice, personalized learning, integrated curricula, and collegial staffing, to name a few.

Take, for example, site-based management, which may be regarded as a "heavy" among the above. For some, it means establishing a building-level team comprised of the principal, teachers, and representatives from the community. Their role is to discuss issues brought to them and then to recommend decision options. For others, it means creating a management team of the principal, teachers, and community members and giving it full responsibility for the school's personnel and program budget as well as being accountable for instructional outcomes. These different interpretations of site-based management are only two of many being applied across the country under the rubric of restructuring. I know of one school that considered its effort to expand the school day from seven periods to eight as restructuring. Clearly, the term continues to mean different things to different persons.

For most educators, restructuring means some form of school reform, such as the Effective Schools Movement of the past decade. Yet for another, smaller group, restructuring connotes not reform, that is, improving what essentially is already in place, but radical *transformation*, a substantive, *systemic* change in the structure of education itself. It is the latter interpretation, I believe, that addresses most clearly the nature of the changes that will be required if we are to provide the quality of education needed for the future. This fastback will examine aspects of restructuring from this perspective.

First, however, let me clarify how I am using the terms "restructuring," "redesigning," and "systemic." If structure consists of the interdependent parts of an organization, then restructuring requires us to examine those interdependent parts to see how they are related. "Systemic," a yeasty term current in the literature of restructuring, refers to the interrelatedness of parts to each other and to the whole. As we shall see, it is a term that is central to the whole idea of restructuring. The term "redesign" refers to the arrangement of elements that make up a structure. I find it helpful to think of restructuring as providing the conceptual framework, or the "Why" and the "What," and of redesigning as the "How" and the "So What." (What will it look like? How will all of the elements fit together and work in harmony? Will it really make a difference?)

In terms of the individual school, structure may include at least the following:

- How essential beliefs and values regarding learning are agreed upon and manifested by all of its stakeholders.
- How the school is managed.
- How the school is staffed.

- How instruction is organized.
- How learning settings are designed and resources are made available.
- How learning time serves the needs of clients (students).

My focus for restructuring-redesign is the individual school. Its vital signs can be confirmed only by the quality of learning that occurs in the lives of individual students in those places called school. Yet, it is fair to say that most of what will be proposed in the ensuing pages is not likely to take place without a mix of supportive legislation, specific state variances, gutsy school boards, superintendents, principals (acting together), committed staff persons and, where needed, the endorsement of teacher associations/unions.

If comprehensive, nationwide, educational restructuring is to occur, it will have to be through a very different set of relationships and agreements yet to be fashioned among the major stakeholders in the education establishment. And to fashion these new relationships and agreements will require a head-on confrontation with current bureaucratic structures in education.

Bureaucracy, to cite a definition provided by Warren Bennis (1969), a pioneer in organization development, includes at least the following components:

- A well-defined chain of command.
- A system of procedures and rules for dealing with all contingencies relating to work activities.
- A division of labor based on specialization.
- Promotion and selection based on technical competence.
- Impersonality in human relations.

In the ensuing pages it will be evident that whatever the emerging structure of schooling for the 21st century becomes, it likely will be at odds with the conventional elements of bureaucracy described above. Simply stated, the stuff of school restructuring/redesign represents the antithesis of conventional bureaucratic organization.

Although restructuring tends to have a future focus, our redesigning process must engage the present. The reality is that there still are in excess of 75,000 school facilities designed expressly for an outmoded, cell-bell, industrial model of schooling. Visioning what a school might look like for the 21st century surely ought to be different from what it might have been three generations ago. How do we move toward a yet undefined, indeterminate educational structure and, while so doing, engage a futures-oriented, systemic change process in our schools?

In this fastback I shall describe a way of accomplishing this transition at the individual school level. It involves a feasible procedure for redesigning today's schools into houses of 100 to 150 students, each with collegial staff teams of 4 to 6 teachers (and whatever additional support persons may be available). These multi-aged student groups and transdisciplinary staff are housed in functional and contiguous "task-based" spaces remodeled from 4 to 6 conventional classrooms. Interrelated elements attended to within this redesign process include the personalizing of learning, alternative and comprehensive assessments of learning outcomes, student-staff roles and relationships, parent-school partnerships, integrated curricula, instructional strategies, and time and space use.

Why a Need to Restructure-Redesign?

Over the past century, schools have reflected the requirements of a society moving from an agricultural to an industrial way of life. Operating on a seasonal basis from September to June, it was anticipated that students, planted in September's soil, would grow, ripen, and be harvested the following June, and subsequently replanted the following fall for further education. Through the agricultural era, uprooting from the schooling soil came early for most students. Fewer than 10% of America's young people attended beyond grammar school at the turn of the twentieth century.

With the twentieth century came the industrial age, where most persons could expect to be engaged in one vocation or career throughout their adult work life. That vocation or career represented stability. With the industrial way of life, schooling design took on the factory look. As Alvin Toffler (1984) expresses it: "[S]ocial inventors believing the factory to be the most advanced and efficient agency for production, tried to embody its principles in other organizations as well. Schools, hospitals, prisons, government bureaucracies, other organizations thus took on many of the characteristics of the factory — its division of labor, its hierarchical structure and its metallic impersonality."

Combining agricultural and industrial characteristics, the structure of conventional schooling sustained its seasonal schedule and emphasized standardization, specialization, synchronization, and centralization. To this day our language refers to students as the *resources* of our country and the *products* of our educational system. As one student aptly put it, "Education is like dog food. The buyers aren't the eaters!"

Over the past three decades, our industrial society has been rapidly displaced by the Information Age. Marked by the emergence of high technology and a global economy, this new age presents a formidable challenge to our conventional approaches to schooling. Economic and social trend data now address the need for improving students' thinking skills, of strengthening students' self-directedness and the ability to take responsibility for their own learning. Its essence is continuing, lifelong learning. Perhaps as important is the need for every student to learn how to protect the environment they share with all other human beings on this Planet Earth.

Therefore, the ethos of future schooling must reflect diversity rather than standardization, decentralization rather than centralization. And rather than continued specialization, particularly in the professions, people must be generalists, adaptive and flexible, able to cope with conditions even more unstable and stressful than those of current times. Civic roles must be expanded to include caretaker of our planet.

There is a fundamental difference between efforts to improve schooling by *refining* existing practices (fine-tuning the mechanism) and restructuring schooling practice (redesigning and realigning the structure's major elements at the individual school level). The former calls for simply doing better what is presently being done and reflects the attitude, "If it ain't broke, don't fix it." The latter calls for a major transformation of the structure and reflects the attitude, "It may not be broken, but is it really the best design to ensure the quality of learning necessary for young people who will be adults in the 21st century?"

While we surely need to envision a host of far-ranging options for education two or three generations hence, it is the present that demands our attention. In a very real sense, that future is now. Thousands of schools across the country are designed like factories, organized like factories, and still function like factories. However well-intentioned and caring the teachers or administrators (and there are many), the system takes its toll on too many students. At its root, it is an issue of design. What needs to be done now is to move from a too comfortable accommodation with the present factory model school to a more personalized redesign better reflecting the needs of all students.

Limitations of the Existing "Classroom-Isolated" Teacher Model

A simple illustration is useful here to clarify why a comprehensive schooling redesign requires a change in the conventional classroom model, as well as demonstrating the ongoing interplay of design elements in any school setting. Some years ago, as a state consultant, I had occasion to visit a teacher in her middle elementary classroom. The teacher (I'll call her Ms. Jones) had asked me to bring some resource materials as well as to visit with her during lunch while she shared some of her students' work applying divergent thinking strategies. I arrived earlier than expected, with about 15 minutes to spare until lunch. Ms. Jones was working in one corner of the room with a group of about 10 students, listening to them read one at a time. She invited me to take a chair and then resumed her work with the group.

About a dozen students were sitting at desks, grouped by fours, doing seatwork in what I would term a "holding pattern." Within a few minutes of my arrival, one young lad waved his hand vigorously until he had Ms. Jones' attention. She interrupted her work with the group and invited the boy to speak. He asked if he might use the clay, which was kept in boxes by the window. Perhaps because of my presence, perhaps because she wished to demonstrate a flexible response to a perceived student need, Ms. Jones responded with a nod.

The boy (I'll call him Burt) went to the box, secured a large ball of gray clay, and proceeded to mold it by pounding it vigorously against the surface of the desk. Thump-Thump-Thump. This caught the attention of everyone, including Ms. Jones and her reading group. She lifted her eyes and with a hand signal indicated that Burt ought to try to be a bit less noisy. I suspected she already was aware that she had made a questionable choice at the outset. Burt resumed his activity, now with more eyes on his efforts. Easily a third of the reading group were engaged with Burt's task rather than their own. Predictably, the ball of clay found its way to the floor, rolling under an adjacent table some eight or ten feet away. Ms. Jones and Burt's eyes met once again, and his eyes responded, "I don't know how it happened, but could I go get it?" With a perceptible sigh and a nod, she indicated, "Yes," and then gently but firmly said to Burt, "Don't you think it would be a good idea to put the clay back for now? There'll be time later to use it." And he willingly acquiesced. Ms. Jones closed down the reading group and then prepared the class for its departure for lunch.

Later that afternoon as I motored home, I reflected on what I had observed in those brief moments in Ms. Jones' room. She had been attempting to work interactively with a small group; Burt at the same time and in the same space had been attempting to work at a spatial, kinesthetic task. The remaining students presumably had been attempting to work independently at seat work. I say "attempting" because I was unsure whether they were truly engaged in what they were supposed to be doing.

Ms. Jones had been trying to be all things to all people at the same time, simultaneously managing the direct learning of her reading group and monitoring those in the holding pattern. Wouldn't it have made more sense if Ms. Jones had been able to work interactively, as coach and facilitator, with her reading group without distraction or interruption? Wouldn't it have been helpful if there were a separate space designed to facilitate spatial-tactile learning with its noise, mess, and movement. Of course, we could hire aides to take care of an individual student's request rather than interrupting Ms. Jones in her reading group. But that would require additional money, and it still wouldn't resolve Burt's distracting thump-thump-thump. Nor would it solve the space needs for other kinds of tactile, kinesthetic activity.

Students require different kinds of space designed for different functions. Yet, Ms. Jones' room is *her* room. It has her name on the door. Given her creativity, it likely will be used throughout the day, and for specific periods of time, for a variety of learning tasks. However, it's no secret that Ms. Smith down the hall likes to keep things in order and students apart. So most activity in her classroom employs paper and quiet seat work. The students are grateful for recess.

Most elementary and secondary teachers face the task of orchestrating, minute by minute throughout the day, their respective enterprises (usually in isolation from other staff). Practically all student activity hinges on the baton of the teacher, signaling start-stop, do this-do that, move here-move there, this way-not that way, now be quiet-now you may speak. Is it any wonder that by the end of first grade, youngsters know that when the teacher leaves the room, the baton has gone and order with it. Though good teachers work persistently at encouraging self-discipline, the few times that children have to practice it is when the authority leaves the room; the remainder of the time that umbilical cord between student and teacher is very short, and usually very taut. It confirms control. The present conventional classroom model makes it difficult for students to acquire self-directedness in terms of time management and task commitment.

The example of the schooling redesign described later in this fast-back is not unique, nor is it the only way to transform an existing factory-box-classroom model into something that more clearly serves learning for every student. Certain of its design elements presently are being implemented in schools across the nation as well as abroad. They make sense and they work. However, the design must be regarded as transitional. No one yet has the clairvoyance to envision what schooling will look like 50 years from now, perhaps not even 25 years from now. But to get from here to there in our visioning, we first must take charge of change in the present. Today's schooling will not undergo a restructuring process by itself. At the same time, whatever restructuring we do now, however temporary or transitional, should reflect operationally the best of what is known today about human learning and about those environments and procedures that will enhance it for every student.

The major schooling redesign issues involved in getting from here to there are summarized below.

Industrial Age School Emphases (Need to move from this)	Information Age Schooling Emphasis (Toward this)
1. Top-down organizational structure at state, district levels.	1. Decentralization of decision making, participative management, reduction of federal/state regulations, decisions made closest to where action is carried out, clear accountability.
2. Conventional K-12 curriculum (ages 6-18), proliferation of course titles and fragmented curricula, textbook oriented.	2. Earlier, more flexible entry ages (entry on one's birthday at age 4, 5, or 6), age clustering for instruction (4-7, 8-12, 12-15), simplified core curriculum (less is more), integrative/transdisciplinary approaches, continuing education options, global emphasis on world as interdependent community.
3. Fragmented learning time.	3. Flexible scheduling, variable time blocks.

4. Teacher isolation in planning and instruction, limited planning time.

5. Community involvement in school activities.

6. Classroom (cell) model of organization, by age-grade level.

7. Tracking and ability grouping.

8. Minimal teacher expectations and parental aspirations for disadvantaged/at-risk students.

9. Promotion based on time spent in school, with little evidence of true accomplishment.

10. Teaching stresses low cognitive skills, short-term memory tasks.

11. Student as passive consumer of information.

4. Staff organized as teams for planning and instruction, block of time for team/individual planning.

5. Community/school shared ownership and accountability for carrying out school's purposes.

6. House model design, learning task spaces, multi-age and multi-year student cohort families, school as experiential place.

7. Personalized programming for every student, varied groupings based on task demands and student interests.

8. High expectations for optimal learning of every student.

9. Promotion based on performance, using obtainable outcomes with agreed-on standards.

10. Higher-order reasoning, problem-solving skills.

11. Students as active participants in formulating and accomplishing relevant (real life) objectives.

12. Impersonal student-teacher relationships, emotional flatness of classroom.

12. Teacher as mentor, coach, learning facilitator providing timely feedback to improve student performance; concern for affective needs of students.

13. Flatness in teachers' salary, professional growth options.

13. Differential staffing, salary based on roles and responsibilities.

14. Piecemeal tinkering of present structure, focus on maintaining status quo.

14. Systemic approach to organizational change that transforms school.

Using Strategic Planning
in the Restructuring Process

Like the Minnesota farmer we need to plan our work, then work our plan. Earlier we probably would have used a conventional long-range planning process in which we begin by asking: "What things are we doing now that need to be improved so that five years from now we can show evidence that we are doing them better?" Strategic planning, on the other hand, asks: "Given our best current information about demographic, economic, and organizational factors shaping our society and the world, how should we redesign our schools to enable our youth to engage life more successfully and more health-fully now and as adults?" And a second question would be: "What do we know about human learning that might reinforce a need to redesign our schools?" The former seeks to refine what is. The latter seeks to envision what is *possible*, that is, how schools ought to function in the full service of their students.

To expedite a change process of this magnitude at the individual school level, it is necessary for the strategic planning process to have already been initiated at the school board and district leadership level. Involved in the planning would be representatives from all community constituencies: parents, interested citizens without children in the schools, local business and industry, the professions, high school students, former recent graduates, teachers, principals, and higher education leaders if available. Their activities should include:

1. Gathering and analysis of pertinent local, national, and global trend data (demographic, economic, organizational) likely to have an impact on future educational needs of all of the community.
2. Reaching agreement on those essential learning outcomes requisite to successfully engaging the future.
3. Study and discussion regarding what is known about human learning, as well as factors and conditions that enhance it.
4. Engaging in visioning how the community's schooling might be redesigned to ensure optimal conditions for learning and the achievement of essential learning outcomes for every student, at all ages.
5. Developing, through a synthesis of the above activities, a mission statement that will serve as both an indication of commitment and a call to action for carrying out the district's vision for restructuring its educational program.

A few caveats regarding the strategic planning process are in order here. School districts across the nation, caught up in the fervor of strategic planning, have invested substantial amounts of time and money organizing committees or task forces and then meeting, meeting, meeting. Frequently, this process culminates in the creation of mission statements looking suspiciously like goal statements of the Great Accountability Movement in the early Seventies. What often happens in the writing of the mission statement is that exciting visions for future schooling generated in the earlier stages of the planning process get muddled or lost in the language of conventional goal statements.

Furthermore, it has to be acknowledged that a good share of a school district's strategic planning efforts remain "top down." In some districts those persons representing the formal/informal power structure give the illusion of engaging in participative management by holding interminable planning meetings. However, if and when meetings do move beyond that stage of analysis-paralysis, what emerges may be merely incentive grants for school-level "improvement projects." Such projects, at best, serve cosmetically to upgrade existing practice, yet typically shy away from efforts directed toward substantive, systemic change. And that is the issue!

So, how do we transform egg-crate, cell-bell, lockstep structures to be responsive to the demands of future schooling? Surely not by putting braces on a brontosaurus! Having said all of that, it also must be acknowledged that, according to the Gallup/Phi Delta Kappa Polls of the Public's Attitudes Toward the Public Schools, a majority of parents across the nation believe that, although schools nationally need improvement, the schools in their own community are doing quite a good job and deserve an above-average grade. It would appear, then, that there is no broad-based, grassroots mandate for a substantive transformation of American education. However, it does suggest that much more information attending to trend data on major factors shaping the future of our society and to research of the nature of learning will need to reach those constituencies whose participation is vital to this restructuring process.

Circumventing Potential Glitches in Strategic Planning/School Restructuring

When launching a comprehensive school-level redesign, several things can be done to reduce the likelihood of major breakdowns along the way.

First and foremost, this is a people process. Take time to secure a good reading on the interpersonal communications among staff as well as the out-of-school constituencies involved. It is not safe to assume that this process of restructuring will so energize and engage staff and community that old wounds or discontent will disappear. Given the stresses inherent in initial change efforts of this scope, old problems or issues dividing staff/community may, indeed, be exacerbated.

21

Establish and cultivate an authentic partnership with all constituencies involved. The term "involvement," as used in the past, conveys to many, particularly parents, images that are at odds with the long-term process of redesign. All constituencies must feel they are engaged in a mutual, collaborative effort with real ownership of the educational purposes and outcomes sought. Clearly, new and creative avenues for parent and community participation must be identified if the term "partnership" is to have any real meaning.

View this restructuring process as an evolving one. Rather than a linear process with hard timelines and expectations for a product on a given date, phase in the instructional-physical redesign gradually. In schools of more than 500 students, it may take a period of five to eight years to effect systemic change. For smaller schools, three to five years ought to be feasible, given community ownership, staff-administrative stability, and a reasonably positive relationship between school and community.

Phase in systemically. This may be the most difficult to accomplish; but without careful attention to it, the integrity of the redesign plan may be jeopardized. To illustrate, consider the following design elements, which are cited in the literature as descriptors of genuine restructuring:

1. Site-based management and decision making with budgetary control (particularly for personnel), coordinated by a design management team representing all those constituencies previously mentioned.
2. Collegial, team-based staffing.
3. Integrated core curriculum ensuring acquisition of essential, life-serving knowledge and skills by every student. For most schools this will require increasing opportunities for experiential, transdisciplinary learning and for apprenticeships and community service activities.
4. Personalized learning plans for each student designed to a) strengthen their development as responsible, self-directed

persons, b) acknowledge their individual learning styles and preferences, and c) honor and celebrate the ways they give special meaning to their learning through demonstration of individual talents or intellectual strengths.

5. Flexible use of learning time and space, responsive to individual and group task demands.

Now, the first challenge is to phase in a subset of staff and students (a team of 4 to 5 staff and 100 to 150 students). Think of this subset as microcosm (a temporary school within a school), which ought to engage at least all of the above descriptors. To attempt to implement or insert each of the above elements, one or two at a time, year by year, compromises their necessary systemic function. They not only reinforce each other, they require each other. To treat them incrementally is to tinker with the structure rather than transform it.

The act of phasing in successive microcosms of staff and students is as close to systemic change as one is likely to get. But to attempt to implement the redesign of an entire conventional school at one fell swoop, say within a given year, may be courting disaster. There is a rare exception. In a situation where a school district is building a new school, implementation of schoolwide redesign may be feasible given several important conditions: a) the new school's design has been developed through the strategic planning process, b) staffing is voluntary and hand-picked, and c) there has been at least a year of pre-planning prior to occupancy.

There is another exception when schools are remodeled. Each year thousands of older school facilities undergo major renovations. This presents an opportune time to initiate the implementation of systemic redesign by ensuring that the physical upscaling of the old facility helps to carry out the redesign plan with respect to space utilization. Unfortunately, this often fails to happen. I recall sadly visiting a large suburban school district in which a 50-year-old school had been refurbished at a cost in excess of a million dollars. With new wiring, plumbing, paint, carpeting, lighting fixtures, and a computer lab, the school now was a cosmetically upscaled factory school fresh out of the Forties. What went on in that refurbished school in terms of educational programming remained essentially the same, except for the computers.

Keep the ideas of decentralization and personalization in the forefront. By doing this, it helps to ensure that the school will function less like a factory and more like the caring, personalized setting it ought to be. While small schools ought to exhibit less impersonality associated with large schools, even in small schools the instructional design and practices often can reflect a mechanistic mode common to large schools. Dividing a school into "houses" helps to decentralize and to personalize. Collegial staff teaming helps to integrate the curriculum. Together they represent the twin pillars of the new design.

Restructuring Schools Through a House Design

The house design offered here is as an example of a work in progress, not a finished product. Clearly, it is not a static model to be cloned; but it does give evidence of functioning well as a transitional approach in moving a school out of a conventional, lockstep system toward the envisioned ideal of personalized, self-directed, optimal learning for every student.

Whether a school is large (2,000 students) or small (200 students), there are sound, practical reasons for redesigning it into decentralized "houses," each of approximately 125 to 150 students staffed by a four- or five-member collegial team. This design is not a rerun of the earlier "open space" approach. In fact, it is at odds with that earlier design in that the removal of walls as a means of "opening up" learning ignored the range of learning styles and preferences of students it served as well as the systemic aspects of the changes accompanying it.

Learning space in this design is not neutral. It is functional, task-based, and learner-centered. The house, with its family of students, provides an environment for a healthy student-support system as well as a place where teachers can connect with students and other staff in a far more personal manner than the conventional classroom cell model. The unity of the teaching team is balanced nicely with the diversity of professional roles engaged in by the individual staff, as coaches, facilitators, and presenters of selective, didactic instruction.

The Process of Implementing the House Model

Several preconditions are critical to the implementation of the house model:

1. The school board and administration must publicly acknowledge ownership of and commitment to the venture.
2. A "critical mass" of staff at the participating school must indicate strong support for a comprehensive restructuring effort.
3. There must be a knowledgeable, school-community support group willing to become partners in this long-term change process.
4. The leadership responsible for directing the process for effecting such significant change must be committed to attending to the "person" needs of all constituencies affected by it.

The individual school must serve as the seedbed for this grassroots process. Although authorization and support from school district leadership are essential to the success of this process, it is not likely to acquire healthy roots through administrative mandate or school board directive. Rather, it will require a "critical mass" of an individual school's staff, the principal, and an active parent support group.

How many is a critical mass of staff? In every school there is likely to be a small number of dissonant staff who will welcome an opportunity to leave the lockstep model of conventional schooling. Organizational development experts called these persons "variance sensors." They sense the constraints of the mindless periodicity of the day's schedule and the isolation imposed by the classroom cells they inhabit. They are aware that many of their students have educational and personal needs that are not being addressed. They are aware that tinkering with the system through more staff-development courses has not served to transform the structure on behalf of students.

Every school also is likely to have another small number of staff who take comfort in remaining as masters within their own territory, their classroom. It is their turf. They adamantly oppose any change disrupting the status quo. Although they may argue for fewer students, more materials, and a reduction of regulations imposed from above, they view the system as working adequately for them. They have paid their dues by going through training programs in which they usually sat, listened, took notes, and responded to questions. Now they are in charge. They have knowledge to impart and they wish their students to succeed. If only students would listen — and learn.

Making up the middle are a majority of staff, open to change but needing more time to think through the details and implications of any departure from the present routine. Given time, say over a period of five years, most will become excited about and responsive to what this kind of redesign might do for students and for them. They are the latent strength for systemic change; but they will not buy into the change design without time for awareness raising, which may eventually lead to commitment.

It makes sense, therefore, to begin with that "critical mass," while at the same time providing time and opportunity for the remainder of the staff to observe and discuss the redesign plan. With sufficient information, they will be less likely to try to "shoot it down" before it becomes operational. Over the course of five years or so, as the efficacy of the new design is confirmed, the entire school would be organized into houses.

While the pilot house functions initially as a school-within-a-school, it does so only as a stage in the phasing-in process. Creating a permanent "alternative" school within a conventional school is not recommended. It could create division among students and tends to send a message to the community that the alternative school is for those who cannot make it in the mainstream (even if the mainstream is subtly stifling the student growth it purports to serve). A school needs to be at one in its vision and values regarding learning.

House Organizational Characteristics

A redesigned school with several houses designed for personal learning might include the following characteristics:

1. Each student has a personal learning plan representing two weeks to several months of anticipated work, depending on student maturation.

2. Students may function in cross-aged groups if deemed appropriate for their personal learning needs.

3. Student advisories (small groups of students, each with its personal academic advisor) provide interpersonal as well as academic support systems for every student.

4. Each house staff team of 4 to 5 teachers, plus support personnel, has full responsibility for program and budget, with support from the school's design management team.

5. In an elementary school, house teams may be organized vertically to include two or three conventional grade levels. Secondary school house teams initially may work best as cross-disciplinary teams within a given grade level or, more ambitiously, vertically across grades 9-12.

6. House teams in elementary schools are curriculum generalists but each member also has a concentration in a major core curriculum area. At the secondary level, staff expand their professional repertoire beyond their content speciality area in order to function as generalists as well.

7. Student progress is measured by performance (know-how, know why, and can-do) rather than on the basis of age or time engaged. A journal, portfolio, and other information on student progress are maintained by each student.

8. House spaces are designed for functional, on-demand use by students, with varied work stations suited for specific tasks.

9. Curricula honor both transdisciplinary as well as intradisciplinary learning.

10. Learning time is flexible and is based more on student task needs than on a fixed schoolwide schedule. Scheduling on demand is feasible because of the small numbers of students within a house. At the secondary level, computer capabilities make it possible for individual students to schedule learning time in the "out-of-house" learning spaces throughout the building where the technology/equipment is located.

Phasing in the Change

A phasing-in process over a period of three to five years, during which appropriate staff development occurs, provides time for staff teams to internalize and "own" the redesign plan. Although a best scenario might envision an elementary school of 500 students moving through this process of change and implementing three or four fully functioning houses over a period from five to eight years, this is assuredly not a straight-line, linear process of change. Conventional, long-range planning expectations often fly out the window in pulling off systemic change. As one principal involved in developing a house model put it, "It's a struggle learning to juggle." He was attempting to support a pilot group, respond to a second team that wished to initiate its house but clearly was not ready, and at the same time was experiencing dissension from a small core of conventionalists.

It often is a struggle for the pilot team to get a handle on all the design elements and to engage them systemically so they fit together in the overall design plan. This again points up the need to take time to plan carefully before putting that first house into operation. Certainly, one should not expect all of the design elements to be humming harmoniously in the first phase. They won't be. But once the systemic skeleton defining the intent is in place, then the refining process can occur.

Central to the refining process will be staff development. The staff-development needs within each house will be different and vary in length. With the house design, staff development can be personalized by team, and even within teams. Rather than being incremental, staff development will be systemic, creating a synergy of effect.

Putting the Pieces Together at the Individual School Level

Seven basic interrelated elements are basic to the planning needs of schooling, whether conventional or restructured. They are: 1) purposes, 2) students, 3) strategies, 4) stuff, 5) staff (including support personnel), 6) space, and 7) time. The teacher in a conventional classroom must control all these elements simultaneously every day. Typically, they manage a large group of students in isolation from colleagues and orchestrate resources and time to respond to class needs each day. At the elementary level, classroom environmental constraints dictate, in large measure, who will do what, when, and where. It is not an environment likely to extend student self-directedness or to be responsive to the range of student differences. At the secondary level the schedule, with its mindless periodicity, moves students from feeding pen to feeding pen in increments of time that often have little to do with the nature of the learning task at hand. Digression from the schedule occurs only when the principal elects to make it happen, or the school's athletic successes demand it.

By contrast, consider what would happen if curricula, staff roles, space, and time were redesigned with the goal of encouraging optimal student learning. In a house design model in an elementary school, the house might be made up of five former contiguous classrooms, which have been remodeled to provide distinct spaces for a variety of learning tasks. The synergism of this design makes it possible for every student to have a range of personal learning options in diverse settings. The staff team functions in various roles. Learning time is flexible depending on the task. Similarly, at the secondary level, the staff is organized into four- or five-member core curricular teams who occupy contiguous space redesigned to meet varied task needs of students. Specialized learning areas and their staffs (art, physical education, shops, etc.) remain as they are, and students go to them from their decentralized houses.

Now let's consider what the seven basic elements of schooling would look like in the house design model.

Purposes. What desired learning outcomes might be strengthened through a house design model? Some examples are:

- Self-directedness in initiating and accomplishing relevant learning.
- Sense of self-worth and confidence resulting in continued personal and academic growth.
- Mastery of essential knowledge, concepts, and thinking skills.
- Working cooperatively with other students and adults and contributing to others' success.
- Creativity in problem identification and problem solving.
- Nurturing of one or more specific talents or performance areas.

Students. What is known about human development and learning that might justify our efforts in redesigning our school and its processes/procedures? Consider the following thoughts about learning as expressed by social psychologist Goodwin Watson (1960):

We learn only what is appropriate to our purposes.

We learn only in relation to what we already know.

We learn when there is freedom from discouragement, the expectation of failure, or threat to physical, emotional, or intellectual well-being.

Whatever is to be learned will remain unlearnable if we believe that we cannot learn it or if we perceive it as threatening.

Novelty is generally rewarding.

We learn best that which we participate in selecting and planning ourselves.

Genuine participation (as compared with feigned participation to avoid punishment) intensifies motivation, flexibility, and rate of learning.

31

An autocratic atmosphere produces increasing dependence on the authority, with consequent obsequiousness, anxiety, shyness, and acquiescence.

The best time to learn anything is when it is perceived to be immediately useful to us.

"Closed" authoritarian environments condemn most learners to continuing criticism, sarcasm, discouragement so that self-confidence, aspiration, and a healthy self-concept are destroyed.

"Open," non-authoritarian environments are conducive to learner initiative and creativity, encouraging the learning of attitudes of self-confidence, originality, self-reliance, enterprise, and independence.

Strategies. What instructional and organizational strategies might be initiated or strengthened through a redesign of our school and its processes/procedures? Examples include: student-staff advisories, cooperative learning, peer tutoring, cross-age student grouping, use of mentors/tutors, task grouping, house staff theme seminars.

Stuff. In what ways might a schooling redesign expand as well as strengthen the application of resources, both human and material? Examples include: allocating space for active learning throughout the curriculum; having on-demand access to computers and other telecommunication technology, thus reducing the present paper blizzard of ditto sheets whose content too often offers only "bits and pieces" learning.

Staff. In what ways might staff and support personnel be deployed to serve students more effectively and efficiently? Examples include a differentiated staff with credentialed professionals responsible for curriculum and supervision of students' personal learning plans and non-certified staff to respond to specific needs of students, such as individual tutoring or supervising task groups and student advisories.

Space. In what ways might spaces be redesigned and redefined in order to provide areas conducive to various learning tasks? Examples include spaces for groups of students to interact with the teacher without auditory or visual distraction, spaces for spatial-tactile-kinesthetic learning, spaces for quiet reading, and spaces for more independent, self-directed learning.

Time. In what ways might time be allocated so that it is appropriate for the nature of the learning task? The house design model lends itself to flexible scheduling of time for group work, science experiments, projects, field trips, etc., without the constraints of a school's master schedule. If two hours or two days are needed for a particular learning task, it is possible to plan the time to fit the task.

All seven of these elements must be considered when initiating school redesign. They can be used for "planning down" and then "implementing up." However, the staff must have a clear grasp of the inter-relationships of these seven elements before undertaking any restructuring of the physical environment.

Benchmarks Toward
Implementing School Redesign

It would be misleading to assume that a process of school redesign follows in a neat, sequential order. Timelines and expectations are approximations at best. Yet from the experience of those schools that have undertaken systemic change with positive results, we can identify benchmarks of their success from the decisions and subsequent actions they took along the way. The benchmarks follow.

1. *Translating the district mission statement at the school level.* Each school staff and its constituents need to have confirmation of the district's commitment to change as documented in the district mission statement. In this way their roles in undertaking systemic change in their individual school will be legitimized. Further, the change process at the individual school will be facilitated if representatives of the staff and community members already have been involved in the district's visioning/mission-setting process.

2. *Inviting staff to work cooperatively in studying and discussing the following questions:*

- What ought to be the essential student learning outcomes in order for them to live productively now and as adults in the 21st century?
- What do we know about human learning?
- What conditions for learning are essential to ensure optimal achievement for every student in this school?

- How might our schooling structures be redesigned in terms of the above in order to achieve excellence?

3. *Empowering staff.* Staff engaged in restructuring require, above all else, consistent, supportive leadership, but not in the form of top-down mandates. When an administrator is perceived to be in the role of "giving and taking away," it is difficult to convince staff that they really are trusted or that their efforts are not likely to be summarily ended by a new administrative edict. Empowering staff to engage in collegial planning and cooperative decision making is an early and vital step to successful restructuring. It will all come together when the staff actually design their house model and determine how it will function to serve the learning needs of every student. Empowerment is strengthened as staff realize professional satisfaction from their efforts.

4. *Identifying the critical mass.* If the redesign process is deferred until all staff are convinced of its efficacy, change might never be undertaken. On the other hand, trying to steamroll the change process by administrative fiat will surely cripple the effort. Because the entire process is centered on people, it is critically important to provide a comfort zone within which all staff can have time to sort out its implications and its value to them and their students.

It is unrealistic to expect total staff commitment to school redesign. Move with those ready to go. This initial staff team can undertake the pilot phase of restructuring without alienating or polarizing the rest of the staff. However, it is important that, prior to first-phase activities, the remaining staff indicate a willingness to at least discuss and/or debate the merits of this proposed, long-term restructuring process openly with colleagues. A rule of thumb is that if 65% of the staff is initially willing to tacitly accept the redesigning activities of the pilot staff team, the process may have a reasonable likelihood for implementation over the following five to eight years.

A troubling bottom line is that 15% of a school's staff, even after four or five years, may find themselves incapable of or unwilling to accept the redesign plan. As the whole school moves toward total restructuring, it might be better for these persons to request a transfer to another school with a more traditional program.

5. *Organizing a design management team.* This group serves as the coordinating voice of the school's vision for change. Its membership includes representatives from the pilot staff team as well as additional teachers who hold leadership roles in the school, but who at this point may be uncertain regarding the merits of systemic school redesign. The inclusion of key parents as well as a central office liaison is also important to ensure the continuity and the integrity of the process throughout the five- to eight-year period needed for full implementation. As its membership changes over time, ownership expands and continuing advocacy for the process is strengthened.

6. *Conducting the charette.* The charette is an intensely focused exercise for budding architects, who get together to solve an important problem in architectural design under carefully prescribed conditions. Borrowing the concept for our purposes, the charette becomes a school community's design clinic, during which participants create a first working draft of a school's redesign.

Drawing on information derived from the staff's earlier awareness-orientation-visioning meetings and from the input of the pilot school's design management team, a charette may be carried out in a two-day intensive workshop or conducted over a period of several months. The product is the draft of a working model of a first house, which might be implemented the following year. Subsequent charettes extend the design process to additional school teams over the ensuing three to eight years.

I have found the charette experience to be of pivotal importance within the larger redesign process. It usually is a positive experience for participants, who work in groups of four to six and put into focus all the visioning that has gone on earlier. In essence, participants bring their visions about a redesigned school literally to the drawing board. Some of the stimulus questions used to address the issues related to school redesign are:

In what ways will a redesign of our school specifically serve to strengthen each student's academic and personal growth?

How might we describe a typical student's and teacher's day in our redesigned school?

In what ways will our redesign influence and/or alter the ways in which we presently appraise and evaluate student and staff performance?

What specific changes in relationships with the central office might we anticipate as a result of our redesign?

What existing administrative practices and functions ought to be sustained and strengthened within our schooling redesign?

In what ways will our redesign enhance the sense of ownership of community persons and business and industry relative to leadership, support, and resource roles?

How might staff members function differently in serving students in our redesigned school?

7. *Monitoring concerns at the school level.* From the inception of the decision to engage in restructuring, an ongoing activity is maintaining clear communications with all constituencies affected by this change effort and monitoring the concerns that may arise as the process moves ahead. Schools involved in restructuring have found the Concerns Based Adoption Model (CBAM) to be a useful reference for the development of their own instruments for monitoring and responding to constituents' concerns regarding the design process through all stages from planning through implementation. Further, the model may be helpful in assessing the perceived extent to which the design has been instituted systematically (Hall et al. 1973, 1975).

8. *Assessing progress.* At the outset of the redesign process, criteria should be established as a basis for determining whether the desired conditions for optimal learning have been instituted and whether student learning outcomes are being realized. A major task for the design management team, in collaboration with administration, is to determine what the standards for quality learning are to be and to

ensure that the means of assessing those outcomes reflect the diversity of student talents and interests. These assessments should include, but not be limited to:

a. Student outcome data on such criteria as self-directedness in learning; acquisition of essential skills, concepts, knowledge; self-esteem; flexibility and adaptiveness in responding to problem situations; the ability to work well with others.

b. Design elements identified as critical to the school's restructuring, for example, curricula, staff roles and functions, governance, space and time use, school-community relationships, and resource applications. Some assessment questions might be: To what extent and how well do these elements function systemically to ensure optimal learning for every student? Has curricula been reduced from its previous "cover-all" character? Have those "essentials" (worthy to be learned and retained) been identified and are they presently incorporated within the integrated curricular design both within and across houses? Are staff organized on a differentiated basis? Is there regular representation by community adults, whose particular talents and abilities help to support students?

Summing Up: Where Have We Been, And Where Should We Be Heading?

This fastback has been about educational restructuring, about the present movement to transform its entire form and functions, not mere fine-tuning of the system but a major redesign.

Throughout the last half of this century, it seems that every decade or so we need to create a whipping boy of public education in one form or another. Sputnik set things off in the late Fifties. In the early Seventies it was the accountability movement, and in the recent Eighties we experienced the criticisms of *A Nation At Risk*. And now in the Nineties, playing counterpoint to the restructuring movement, we have a great debate under way as to whether national testing will be necessary to get education back on track.

With each of the movements, including the one currently going on, the criticism has been focused on students. The complaint, in essence, is that students aren't learning, they don't know how to think, and they don't write or compute well. And the corollary to this criticism is that it must be the schools' and/or the parents' fault.

The irony in all these criticisms is that of all those things the human organism does, it is to learn. The healthy human being never has to be taught how to think or learn. Our human brain of 50 billion cells at birth has been marvelously designed to do just that. It is no passive organ. David Loye (1983), in summarizing the work of contemporary investigators, says, "The active thrust of mind is a basic survival mechanism, it operates at all levels from the neurons upward, and that it takes two main forms: searching behavior and exploratory behavior. Searching behavior is what we do when we have a specific need in mind — for food, or sex, or a place to sleep. Exploratory behavior, by contrast, is unspecific. We are simply motivated to keep moving, looking, hearing, feeling by needs for stimulation that are among the most basic for all life forms. These stimuli are almost as necessary for well being as is food or water." What has this to do with schooling?

Formal schooling is relatively recent to the entire human experience, engaging, at most, a modest six thousand years or so of our species lifescape. Fifty thousand years ago, without formal schooling, human beings were contemplating the mystery of death, observing the regularity of seasonal change, worrying about a scarcity of food, and shaping technology to meet their needs. In Loye's language, they were searchers and explorers. As harsh and uncompromising as the environment was, they were able to accommodate to it better than do our youth today.

School restructuring, unlike all of the other movements mentioned above, may represent our best opportunity at the close of this century to create a fundamental shift in the way we view education. Restructuring is not just a "school" issue. The essence of restructuring is societal. We are all in it together. Restructuring has to do not only with systemic changes in the schooling process but also with the desperately needed renewal across the land. Our schools mirror the social order (and disorder) in which they are embedded. The larger society subsumes the school, and the circle cannot be complete without including all the stakeholders.

This generation needs a brief, salient mission statement confirming the 21st century as the Century of the Child. And in the meantime, our aim as educators, in partnership with concerned community persons, must be:

> To direct our collaborative energies to creating and supporting environments that celebrate active, personal learning, for searching and exploring.

To fashion varied learning settings within which the highest quality of learning may take place.

To provide adult support and structure appropriate to each student's maturity.

To ensure that instructional strategies and resources are responsive to each student's unique needs and strengths.

It is a formidable challenge to move from a factory-oriented system of schooling toward a design more in touch with the emerging demands of the 21st century and with the needs and capabilities of each unique human being. But it is not an impossible task. We must be about it. NOW.

References

Bennis, Warren G. *Organization Development: Its Nature, Origins and Prospects*. Reading, Mass.: Addison-Wesley, 1969.

Hall, G.E.; Wallace, R.C.; and Dorsett, W.A. *A Developmental Conceptualization of the Adoption Process Within Educational Institutions*. Austin: Research and Development Center for Teacher Education, University of Texas, 1973.

Hall, Gene E.; Loucks, Susan; Rutherford, W.L.; and Newlove, B.W. "Levels of Use of the Innovation: A Framework for Analyzing Innovation Adoptions." *Journal of Teacher Education* 26, no. 1 (1975): 52-56.

Johnson, Wendell. *Your Most Enchanted Listener*. New York: Harpers, 1956.

Loye, David. *The Sphinx and the Rainbow*. New York: Bantam, 1983.

Toffler, Alvin. *The Third Wave*. New York: Bantam, 1984.

Watson, Goodwin. "What Psychology Can We Feel Sure About?" *Teachers College Record* (February 1960).

stback Titles (Continued from back cover)

PDK Fastback Series Titles

(Continued on inside back cover)